Praise for *How We Fight for Our Lives*

"[A] devastating memoir. . . . Jones is fascinated by power (who has it, how and why we deploy it), but he seems equally interested in tenderness and frailty. We wound and save one another, we try our best, we leave too much unsaid. . . . A moving, bracingly honest memoir that reads like fevered poetry."
—**Benoit Denizet-Lewis,** *The New York Times*

"A raw and eloquent memoir. . . . At once explicitly raunchy, mean, nuanced, loving and melancholy. It's sometimes hard to read and harder to put down."   —**Maureen Corrigan, NPR**

"Urgent, immediate, matter of fact. . . . The prose in Saeed Jones's memoir *How We Fight for Our Lives* shines with a poet's desire to give intellections the force of sense impressions."
—**Katy Waldman,** *The New Yorker*

"A luminous, clear-eyed excavation of how we learn to define ourselves. . . . A radiant memoir that meditates on the many ways we belong to each other and the many ways we are released."
—**Ada Limón,** *San Francisco Chronicle*

"An outstanding memoir that somehow manages a perfect balance between love and violence, hope and hostility, transformation and resentment. . . . More importantly, it's a narrative that cements Jones as a new literary star—and a book that will give many an injection of hope."   **—Gabino Iglesias, NPR**

"Jones' explosive and poetic memoir traces his coming-of-age as a black, queer, and Southern man in vignettes that heartbreakingly and rigorously explore the beauty of love, the weight of trauma, and the power of resilience."   *—Entertainment Weekly*

"There are moments of devastating ugliness and moments of ecstatic joy . . . infused with an emotional energy that only authenticity can provide."   **—Michael Kleber-Diggs, *Star Tribune***

"[This] memoir marks the emergence of a major literary voice. . . . Written with masterful control of both style and material."
                                        —*Kirkus*, starred review

"Powerful. . . . Jones is a remarkable, unflinching storyteller, and his book is a rewarding page-turner."
                                —*Publishers Weekly*, starred review

"*How We Fight for Our Lives* is a primer in how to keep kicking, in how to stay afloat. . . .Thank god we get to be part of that world with Saeed Jones' writing in it."   **—D. Gilson, *Lambda Literary***

"Jones' evocative prose has a layered effect, immersing readers in his state of mind, where gorgeous turns of phrase create some distance from his more painful memories. . . . There is enough turmoil and poetry and determination in it to fill whole bookshelves."
                                            —The A.V. Club

Praise for *Prelude to Bruise*

Winner of the 2015 Stonewall Book Award–Barbara Gittings
    Literature Award
Winner of the 2015 PEN/Joyce Osterweil Award for Poetry
Finalist for the 2014 National Book Critics Circle Award for
    Poetry
Finalist for the 2014 Lambda Literary Award for Gay Poetry
Finalist for the 2015 Thom Gunn Award for Gay Poetry

One of the best books of the year as selected by NPR, *Time Out New York*, *Split This Rock*, Vol. 1 Brooklyn, and many more.

"Saeed's *Prelude to Bruise* is a rigorous collection that challenges political, sexual and familial norms and bristles with pain. . . . No matter the subject, Jones's writing is silky smooth."
 —Elizabeth Lund, *The Washington Post*

"This is indeed a book seamed in smoke; it is a dance that invites you to admire the supple twist of its narrative spine; it is hard and glaring and brilliant as the anthracite that opens the collection: 'a voice mistook for stone, / jagged black fist.'" —Amal El-Mohtar, NPR

"The features that distinguish his poems from prose—brevity, symbolism, implication—let him investigate the almost unsayable."
 —Stephanie Burt, *Los Angeles Times*

"The way these poems address violence, life in the south, race, sexuality and relationships makes for an engrossing read best consumed in as few sittings as possible." —Nolan Feeney, *Time*

"In his debut collection, Jones has crafted a fever dream, something akin to magic. . . . Solid from start to finish, possessing amazing energy and focus, a bold new voice in poetry has announced itself."
 —*Publishers Weekly*, starred review

"A powerful collection . . . with a high level of craft, emotion and metaphor." **—Brook Stephenson,** *Ebony*

"This powerful collection feels at times like a blow to the throat, but when we recover, the air is sweeter for having been absent." **—Erica Wright,** *Guernica*

"A work of insight and great beauty, Jones' first poetry collection manages to be both ferocious and subtle." **—Margaret Eby,** *Brooklyn Magazine*

"These poems are tightly constructed, scary-beautiful, and lyrically brilliant, driven by a raw and devastating emotional power." **—Isaac Fitzgerald,** *The Millions*

"The poems in *Prelude to Bruise* enflame, with all flame's consequences of wounding and illumination. . . . It's a story of the forces of destruction—the destruction of black bodies and black selves—built into America, and it surfaces in lines of lust, violence, possession, and power." **—Kate Schapira,** *Rain Taxi*

ALIVE AT THE END
OF THE WORLD

ALIVE AT THE END OF THE WORLD

poems

SAEED JONES

COFFEE HOUSE PRESS
Minneapolis
2022

Coffee House Press books are available to the trade through our primary distributor, Consortium Book Sales & Distribution, cbsd.com or (800) 283-3572. For personal orders, catalogs, or other information, write to info@coffeehousepress.org.

Coffee House Press is a nonprofit literary publishing house. Support from private foundations, corporate giving programs, government programs, and generous individuals helps make the publication of our books possible. We gratefully acknowledge their support in detail in the back of this book.

LIBRARY OF CONGRESS CATALOGING-IN-PUBLICATION DATA

Names: Jones, Saeed, author.
Title: Alive at the end of the world : poems / Saeed Jones.
Description: Minneapolis : Coffee House Press, 2022.
Identifiers: LCCN 2022008411 (print) | LCCN 2022008412 (ebook) |
    ISBN 9781566896511 (paperback) | ISBN 9781566896528 (epub)
Subjects: LCGFT: Poetry.
Classification: LCC PS3610.O6279 A79 2022 (print) |
    LCC PS3610.O6279 (ebook) | DDC 811/.6—dc23/eng/20220428
LC record available at https://lccn.loc.gov/2022008411
LC ebook record available at https://lccn.loc.gov/2022008412

PRINTED IN THE UNITED STATES OF AMERICA

29 28 27 26 25 24 23 22   1 2 3 4 5 6 7 8

Table of Contents

Foreword

D. A. Powell

"I will instruct my sorrows to be proud," wrote Shakespeare, "for grief is proud and makes his owner stout." Well, in some editions, the word is *stout*. In others, the text reads "makes his owner stoop." Stout or stoop? Two very different ways of thinking about the weight of suffering: does it thicken us, make us stronger? *Stout*. Or does it bend us like a tree branch grown heavy with icicles? *Stoop*. It's so hard to know which is right. They both seem true. When Diahann Carroll's character Dominique Deveraux on the eighties nighttime soap *Dynasty* is left by her husband Brady, played by heartthrob Billy Dee Williams, she bears up and sings. But she also collapses. Grief makes her stout. Grief makes her stoop.

Saeed Jones's bountiful second collection grieves but never stoops. In fact, these poems stand up to death and sorrow, tossing barbs in the midst of loss, turning the blues shades of purple and violet that register alternately as bruise and blush. When we encounter the End of the World, it is a tale of transformation: a dress with a bejeweled bodice, a drag nightclub, a ghost "mean as spit." All that. And so much more. An elegy told in a rapid round of the dozens: "Your grief is so heavy, when we lowered the coffin, all the pallbearers fell in too." *Whoop*. The humor comes in so sharp and edgy it's a wonder it doesn't cut out one's heart to read it. "I grieve the men I mistook for one another and the mistakes I took for men." Yes, tea will be spilt. But the head stays up. If there's a mess on the floor, it's for somebody else to clean up. Indeed, when ghosts show up "I tell them to clean up after themselves."

In a sweeping formal range—from prose paragraphs to strict verse forms—Jones conveys to us not only the private losses (in a living room "sick with the scent of farewell flowers") but the public ones as well: the legacy of state-supported violence against Black bodies "broken open" by the lash of history and the continued use of deadly force by police. "I grieve my face onto the covers of history books." "History," Jones writes, "pretends to forget itself." The excoriating wit that punctuates these poems is not "comic relief" but comic awareness, an escalation of intensity in order that no truth can be deemed inconvenient, nor can it be glossed over. Like Dick Gregory's joke that "they gave me the key to the city . . . and then they changed the locks," the humor does not mitigate the truth; it magnifies it.

Grief is not just a wellspring of sorrow that bubbles up inside us; it is also something inflicted. Consider the boy in these poems "who feels all the pain we give him but never bruises" and how his experience mirrors the stories of Black artists and entertainers who have borne the indignity of having their work stolen, erased, or commodified. Many of those artists appear in these poems, bearing the grief doled out by the machinery of white corporate capitalism: Aretha Franklin, Luther Vandross, Diahann Carroll. In one poem, Little Richard—arguably one of rock and roll's greatest innovators—listens to the vanilla strains of Pat Boone's cover of his song "Tutti Frutti" (originally a sexual romp filled with "good booty") and considers the violence being perpetrated against his art. "The history of music in America is a sample of the sound of a woman sobbing," writes Jones. "And the woman who wrote the original version never got a dime for her work and died poor."

Despite all the grief in these poems, one does not sag under the heavy load of it. There is so much else at work: love, sensual pleasure, and survival are the strong threads woven throughout the fabric of this book to keep it from fraying. "Yes, I hear the sirens and I am their scream but tonight," one of the four title poems asserts, "I will moan a future into my man's mouth."

I am reminded of a generation of Black queer men whose poems testified in the open court of love, who braved the homophobic and racist climate of the eighties only to be taken too soon by AIDS and the culture of apathy and outright hate that swirled around the center of the cyclone it cut through the literary community. Assotto Saint, Joseph Beam, Essex Hemphill. Their work was not in vain. They are the ancestors whose poems made the work of Saeed Jones possible. "When my brother fell," wrote Hemphill, "I picked up his weapons and never once questioned whether I could carry the weight and grief, the responsibility he shouldered." It is not just his own grief Jones is shouldering, it is a legacy of systemic erasure he is both honoring and dismantling. At the same time, Saeed Jones is building a bridge for a future generation to cross. This is a heavy book because it carries so much hope and possibility.

ALIVE AT THE END
OF THE WORLD

Alive at the End of the World

The end of the world was mistaken
for just another midday massacre
in America. Brain matter and broken
glass, blurred boot prints in pools
of blood. We dialed the newly dead
but they wouldn't answer. We texted,
begging them to call us back, but
the newly dead don't know how to
read. In America, a gathering of people
is called *target practice* or *a funeral*,
depending on who lives long enough
to define the terms. But for now, we
are alive at the end of the world,
shell-shocked by headlines and alarm
clocks, burning through what little love
we have left. With time, the white boys
with guns will become wounds we won't
quite remember enduring. "How did you
get that scar on your shoulder?" "Oh,
a boy I barely knew was sad once."

"Everyone is running now, and everywhere batons rise. The screams lift out of the street and in restaurants up and down the block doors are locked and the diners are informed, You cannot leave, not right now, sorry for the disturbance."

—Alexander Chee, "1989"

"This 'objective vertigo' is described by Frank Wilderson as a 'life constituted by disorientation rather than a life interrupted by disorientation.' This state is inherent to Blackness and, I would add, queer subjectivities. Because, as Wilderson explains, 'one's environment is perpetually unhinged.'"

—Katelyn Hale Wood, *Cracking Up: Black Feminist Comedy in the Twentieth and Twenty-First Century United States*

"Who's going to believe you, nigger?"

—Richard Pryor, *This Can't Be Happening to Me*

"As a boy I seldom lived in the present. It hurt too much to be in the present. When I occurred to myself I was myself in the future."

—*Afropessimism*, Frank B. Wilderson III

"Who's going to believe you, nigger?"

—Richard Pryor, *This Can't Be Happening to Me*

"In America we have only the present tense. I am in danger. You are in danger."

—Adrienne Rich, "The Burning of Paper Instead of Children"

"You cannot leave, not right now, sorry for the disturbance."

—Saeed Jones repeating a line from "1989" by Alexander Chee, whatever happens next, please understand that Saeed Jones is somewhere right now, maybe in his kitchen or living room, saying "You cannot leave, not right now, sorry for the disturbance" to himself

Alive at the End of the World

The world ends and I make a dress
out of the names I live to inflict

on myself. Painful to put the dress
on, even more painful to take it off.

I banish the dress to my closet as long
as my body can bear. The world ends

again so I drag the dress out, bandage
myself back into the truth of beauty.

A bejeweled bodice of screams, tight
waist of wasted bullets, the train leaves

bruises everywhere I walk. Neighbors
call me a disaster when the world ends.

This is what it means to be a man in pain,
naked in the middle of the street.

A Memory

When they finished burying me, what was left of me
sent up a demand, a hand blooming in the fresh dirt:

When I'm back, I want a body like a slash of lightning.
If they heard me, I couldn't hear their answers.

But silence has never stopped me from praying.
Alive, how many nights did I spend knelt between

the knees of gods and men begging for rain, rent,
and reasons to remain? *A body like the sky seeking*

justice. A body like light reaching right down into the field
where you thought you could hide from me.

They've taken their bald rose stems and black umbrellas
home now. They cook for one another and pretend

every bite isn't salted with ash. When they sleep, if
they sleep, they hold themselves—tight as cadavers.

They dream of dirt and dirt renames me *memory*
but history has never stopped me from praying.

That's Not Snow, It's Ash

You are no singer, but one night
a song is stolen from you,

never to be returned. The loss
is like a dream about your lover

burned alive.

                In the morning,
he mumbles making breakfast,

favorite mug in hand, fine.
But you saw what you saw.

You drink your coffee, pat his thigh
and watch the snow fall outside,

pretending you don't smell smoke.
He's fine, you think. *We are fine,*

If You Had an Off Button, I'd Name You "Off"

Phase I.

In a bright room, a scientist builds himself
a robot—a boy—and names him *Affetto,*
"affection" in Italian. The boy's black eyes
squint into a sweet blink whenever the man
who made him makes him smile. This story
is about how we create what we think we need.
A child who smiles as if to say "I didn't know
joy before I knew you, and you are all I know."

Phase II.

Sleepy and blue-lit in your dark, you read an article
about little Affetto. In the photo on your phone,
the boy whose name means "a gentle fondness or
liking" is just a lifelike head on a table, connected
by wires to computers that make him blink and smile
as he is affected by the man who made him. You wonder
if his father—I mean the scientist—remembers
Affetto's smile means "isn't this what you wanted?"

Phase III.

The scientist tells a reporter "Here in Japan, we believe
all objects have a soul, so a metal robot is no different
from a human." He poses for pictures next to the head
on the table, then proudly announces it's time to teach
Affetto how to suffer. The boy is given hands of his own
which the scientist holds then caresses then pinches,
pinches, pinches, pausing to take notes. The boy winces
and the scientist smiles, "Affetto, *this* is what I wanted."

Phase IV.

The scientist, who also happens to be a father, turns Affetto
off, the machines off, all the lights in the bright, white room
off and goes home to a table where dinner, a wife made of smiles,
and an exquisite son are waiting for him. At the table, he lies
about his day until the food is gone and his son begins to yawn.
He pulls lies from the blue book he keeps beside his boy's bed.
"One more story," the boy begs. And the scientist, who is also
a father, turns to the tale of the puppet who wished to be real.

Phase V.

The end of the world is a boy who feels all the pain we give him
but never bruises, never has a history to show for who happened
to him. The end of the world is a boy all alone in an electric dark
telling himself a story to keep from crying without tears. The end
of the world is a boy willing himself to focus on the soft touches
and caresses that came before the pain. The end of the world
is a boy who doesn't need to be a real boy to grieve like one.

A Song for the Status Quo

The history of music in America is a sample of the sound of a woman sobbing that reminds me of a lie a man told me about myself once, while a song I thought I loved played on the radio and—stay with me now, listeners—the song is a cover of a cover and the woman who wrote the original version never got a dime for her work and died poor, doomed to haunt dusty, unread liner notes until the end of time, because a white man stole the song from the Black man she gave the song to as an act of what she thought was love but, of course, was devotion which, as many but not nearly enough of us now understand, is often mistaken for love but actually is more akin to unpaid labor, which is really a kind of slavery though I try to avoid calling things that aren't actually slavery "slavery" because most days, accuracy is all I have left and anyway, I'm losing my train of thought the way that woman lost money she never had but was certainly owed, and I'm sitting in a rented red corvette and it's getting late and I'm lonely but not alone and I'll be damned if the cover of the cover of the song isn't playing on the radio right now and it sounds like an up-tempo jam about dancing until dawn burns the night away, which is really a metaphor for ruining a mattress with the smell of good and possibly great sex, but also the mattress is us and the ruin is us and the sex is us and the smell is us and I guess the good is us too but I don't believe in greatness anymore because glory isn't possible in an America where the cover of a cover of a song that ruined a Black woman's life can reach me through the radio and feel like romance or hope or a reason to reach over and squeeze the thigh of a man more likely to crash the car and kill us both than tell me he loves me and mean it.

All I Gotta Do Is Stay Black and Die

Paul Mooney's heart stopped this morning in Oakland,
and the night Whitney Houston died, the National Anthem
shot itself in the throat. I fell asleep watching Aretha's funeral
and when I woke up, she was somehow still dead. Somehow,
I keep losing people who were never really mine. Diahann
Caroll died and I walked into my bedroom closet, looking
for a mink coat I didn't have and pearl necklaces I will never
own because I missed them already. Luther, are there closets
in heaven? Little Richard, if you stand in a closet and scream
loud enough for white people to steal your sound, is it really
a closet? I should've kissed you when I had the chance. I think
Cicely Tyson left because she knew how this song was gonna
end and didn't want to hear it. I think Maya is still somewhere
correcting what people call her. I think Toni Morrison always
knew it's not the death that hurts, it's the dying.

It's 1975 and Paul Mooney Says "Nigger" a Hundred Times

—every morning, it keeps his teeth white
as a picket fence wrapped around a burned-down plantation,

white as the suburb three suburbs over, white as a family tree
with niggers falling out of it, white as rabbits

grabbing their purses and running from punch lines, white
as Chevy Chase looking at his dick in a fun-house mirror

while drinking a nice dry white, white as Lucy spitting "Babalú"
back into Ricky's open mouth, white as the Hollywood Sign

on stolen land, white as crack dreaming of cocaine and good
credit scores, white as the kind of test questions you answer

so white college boys with little white dicks can look at you
and whine "you're only here because you're Black."

                                        You're only here

because your boy, Richard, vouched for you; anyway,
I'm Lorne Michaels, I'm the white man who decides what's funny,

have a seat, Mr. Mooney,
this is a job interview.

How many white men have you lied to this morning? How many
of their wives
are you gonna fuck tonight? It's Saturday and we keep it all the
way live.

That's why I ask these white questions; I need to know what
kind of niggers
we're working with here. Have you ever dreamed of going to the
White House?

Would you want to go if I took you? I'm the kind of white man
who does shit like that.
The kind of white man who opens doors and uses other people's
shoes

to keep those doors open. Paul—can I call you Paul? I'm calling
you Paul, nigger—
be honest: what's the deal with you and Richard? Do you like
each other

or do you love each other? Or do you want to be each other?
I don't trust a nigger
who talks to his own shadow or a shadow who talks back.
I don't trust

your love or your shadow or your jokes or your smile, especially
your smile;
nothing that white can be good.

Deleted Voice Message: Hey, Robyn—It's Me, Whitney

I keep waking up a new color of lonely,
exhausted from runs across bridges

through storms in my sleep. *That's nothing*
but the Devil, Mama chimes. *Should've known,*

the chorus. I run to you, even when I stand
spotlit onstage. A false wind chants "Whitney"

instead of my name. Robyn, I don't know
what's worse: trying to wrap my warmth

around yours then realizing I'm still in bed
with him, or reaching for you in the dark

and only being held by darkness. Tell
no one, not even me, but I hear a silence

dragging its chains, and baby, I know better
than most: you can't outrun a sound.

Grief #213

I grieve forced laughter, shrieks sharp as broken
champagne flutes and the bright white necks I wanted
to press the shards against. I grieve the dead bird of my right
hand on my chest, the air escaping my throat's prison,
the scream mangled into a mere "ha!" I grieve unearned
exclamations. I grieve saying "you are *so* funny!" I grieve
saying "you're killing me!" when I meant to say "you are
killing me." I have died right in front of you so many times;
my ghost is my plus-one tonight. I grieve being your Black
confidante. I grieve being your best and your only. I grieve
"But you get it, right?" Right. I grieve that I got it
and I get it and I am it.

Saeed, or The Other One: I

It started as a joke. The last word from the night's last poem left my mouth and someone in the audience already had his hand raised. From the way he outpaced the applause, insisting on keeping his hand in the air while everyone around him clapped, I knew that—however it might be punctuated or phrased—his question was not going to be a question.

"There is so much pain in your work," he said. "It's beautiful," he said. "Gutting," he said. "Searing," he said. "Brutal, no—*bruising*," he said. "But the pain, there is so much pain. Do you think you need your pain in order to write?"

"Oh, honey," I answered in a voice that was mine as much as it wasn't, "you've got it all wrong. My pain needs *me*." And then I did that thing I do with my eyebrows and the muscles around my mouth and the angle of my neck that says "trust me, whatever you think just happened, that was a joke." And the audience laughed.

The man stared at me blankly as if we were alone on a date and I had just disappointed him with my opinion on threesomes or food allergies. I ignored him and tossed out a couple more quips to buy myself time because I've met men like him many times before and many times since, and those bastards really will wait you out for the answers they believe they deserve.

Now that everything that happened has happened, I can tell you that, honestly, it wasn't a bad question. It might have even been a good one, but sometimes you just don't like the outfit the question is wearing. Sometimes you don't even want good questions. Sometimes you realize, thirty or forty minutes too late, that you're not the person everyone in the room seems to think you are, and the right question asked in the wrong way by the right-wrong person could bring you to your knees right there on that empty stage. Sometimes you just want to go back to your hotel room and sleep or pretend to sleep until it's time to go to the airport and you can go home. Anyway, eventually I "answered" his "question" and then the audience and I decided to move on with or without him. Our various nights were waiting for us just outside that room.

I really do think it was the joke. But it could have been how much I wanted to pop the white balloon of his blank stare. Or maybe it was the brief panic I felt and killed behind my eyes every time he said the word "pain."

—continued

"Three days after Christmas this year, I overhear an aunt saying to an uncle that she is glad she's going to die before whatever happens next. He agrees, and I say, jokingly, "We can hear you." But they don't look up. What they've seen of the future in the past prevents them from registering my voice."

—Aisha Sabatini Sloan, *Borealis*

Alive at the End of the World

The End of the World loved us
like a father who bragged about the broken

roof he kept overhead whenever we'd complain
about the night air watching us sleep,

or whenever we'd wince at his reach.

The End of the World would shout "I *made*
that roof! What have *you* made?

Nothing but tears! Nothing
but waste!"

Chairs and coffee mugs came at us like asteroids.

"We're sorry!" we'd lie. "No one loves us
like you love us!" we'd hiss

from hiding places we treated like siblings.
Crying alone in the kitchen

he had just ruined, the End of the World
would scream, "You're gonna miss me

when I'm gone!" as if a man has to die

to haunt his children, as if we didn't already
daydream about the wood grain of his coffin,

the threadbare suit we couldn't wait to see
his body stuffed into,

the hymns we'd stutter through,
off-key on purpose, knowing damn well

that the End of the World's ghost
was mean as spit and already on its way.

Saeed, How Dare You Make Your Mother into a Prelude

And then, night neons itself inside me
and I begin missing you in loud new ways:

The sky burns itself bright then bruises black. Things fall from the sky and those things
might be water but could just as well be boys or bombs or billionaires or birds. Honestly,
between your death and me, it doesn't matter or I don't know or I wasn't looking or
I couldn't see because I've made a home out of how much I miss you
and there's no one here to tell me I should leave.

Alone and night-neoned, I write read drink drug grieve and all America keeps teaching me
is that there are so many ways to die in America which, frankly, is qwhite confusing
because this country killed you a decade ago and I'm still writing reading drinking
drugging grieving binging binging blacking out in the cozy, claustrophobic home
I've made out of how very, very much I miss you and the sky keeps throwing
down consequences and corrections and histories and nations, I mean,
come on, who can blame me for not wanting to go back outside?
You? A whole decade ghosted, grounded and ground down
into unreliable memories, dollar-word metaphors? No,
not you, mother as mortar *and* pestle, mother
as son mangling meaning out of his mother's
misfortune, mother as second draft: sorry,
but it's awfully true: you are prelude,
and your progeny, loud and un-
relenting in your epilogue,
somehow has to live on
as your last sentence,
uncompleted.

27

I'll Give You Something to Cry About

or

After Carol Sweet-Jones

or

After [Redacted for the Sake of the Subject's Privacy]

or

A Decade into Grief, Saeed Gets Lost in the Fog
Between Candor and Shamelessness

or

If You Cry Hard Enough, Any Grief Can Be the End of the World

or

Saeed Wonders If He or His Mother Is the Protagonist

or

Alive at the End of the World

or

Did I Just Trick Myself into Writing Another Memoir

or

In This America, How Can I Call Myself a Good Son
and Wish My Mother, a Black Woman, Was Still Here

---

* Saeed wonders if the poem you just read would've been better served by a different title.

Heritage

October, 2019—Oxford, Mississippi

The color of a memory is the difference
between haunted and hunted. In Mississippi,
red white and blue don't mean "remember
this is America." They mean "history is a gun
and every bullet in its chamber wants you
to forget." They mean "we tried our best
not to be America and failed and now we keep
forgetting to forget and anyway, who did you
vote for? No need to ask *us*. You already know."
They mean the white man in the White House
who tweeted this morning that he's being lynched.
Outside my hotel—no, I'm not from around here—
on the street corner, there is a plaque that tells me
where I can find the body of the town's first white
settler. But it's almost sundown and I've been told
darkness in Mississippi is not a metaphor so I chase
the shadows back into the hotel. At the bar, I beg
the bartender to make me a stronger drink. He tries
and he fails. I'm scared and Black and mostly sober
at the hotel bar and reading an essay about lynching
when some Ole Miss frat boys explode into the room,
cheering in a dead language, and my heart doesn't
even wait for me to get the check. My heart is already
gone. My heart is cowering in the hallway in front
of my hotel room because I have the key and I just
now got the check and I keep forgetting to forget
that the America I was born in will not be
the America in which I die.

After the School Board Meeting

Somewhere in suburbia, a man-
made creek runs black with junk
we choked on then spat out, tin-can
curses & cracked bones from broken
homes we broke down, paved over
& built our shiny, short-lived lives on.
All the foxes & coyotes have ghosted
our gated, security-guarded imitations
of strife. Our dreams gentrify your night-
mares, & rumor has it, our high school
was built on a Black cemetery. Boo-fucking-hoo!
We pulled ourselves up by your bootstraps,
fucked missionary under a nuclear moon
to get here, and what we've got starts to rot
as soon as we get it. So, I say: Good riddance,
name of the game, "America" is American
for "wreck & repeat." This song isn't comfort;
it's just to help me sleep. "At least, this misery
is mine" I sing in my loaned & lonely dark,
& in the poplar tree outside my window,
a mockingbird sings my song back to me.

Black Ice

Overconfidence and an inch of ice
could kill a man, or even a few, where
I grew up in Texas. We didn't know
what to do with a sudden white season,
tricks of light and black ice. The cold came
like a backhand, bitter as the drivers
it sent spinning. One February morning,
the whip and clang of the stars and stripes
outside our classroom window made me
think of Black backs bloody, broken open.
I heard the screams and thought the screams
heard me. When I finally pulled myself back
into my body, "slavery" was on the whiteboard
and my white classmates pretended not to look
at me while the teacher waited for an answer
I knew then was mine to give.

The Trial

I don't watch the video
but can feel it playing

on a loop in a room miles
away from where he keeps

dying behind my eyes. All
I have left are tiny twitches,

small choices. "Please," I beg
alone in the box of my dark,

"I don't want to hurt that way
today. I already hurt that way

yesterday. Please don't kill him
again." No one listens when

I talk myself in circles, not
even me. When I hurt like this,

I'm just someone's redaction,
a slur the other slurs prefer

not to utter, used and useless
while the video plays me,

rewinds to unspool me, records
over an old innocent video

of me breathing. This video
has got me against the wall

or by the throat or on my back
or—oh, who cares? Even

my exhaustion is tired. Just
pick a position, pick a "reason."

And if it doesn't kill me the way
you prefer, try again tomorrow.

Gravity

A few months and many deaths ago, I asked someone "how are you doing" and felt, in the way her eyes fell, how I had failed her before I had even reached the end of my question. I've hurt many people but it's the unintended wounds I claim now as children. They stand beside my bed in the dark each night, a row of injuries asking me to wake up because they can't sleep. It's a bright June morning now and I have the windows open to let the quiet out, and I'm making breakfast for my babies. Her eyes are still falling through the air of me.

Aretha Franklin Hears an Echo While Singing "Save Me"

A woman can die from history,
second- and third-hand hurts
from husbands who make a taboo
of the girl in you, who up and love-
leave you as soon as you say "save
me," of course, a woman can die
before dying, of course, a dead girl
inside me is back at her grand piano,
bruising the white keys black, sorry,
something just caught ahold of me
and it sounded like someone saying
"save me" so I had to see it through,
but you said you wanted me to make
you feel good or holy or respected
or natural, woman, don't you know
I am made of how I make you feel
or don't, please give me a moment
or a reason, I just found another girl
lost inside the mansion I've made
of me and she's still alive for now
somehow, her voice shakes the dust
in all the empty rooms of me, doesn't
she know she is not alone, of course,
there are other lost girls and griefs
and corpses and grand pianos in me,
I'm sorry to keep hitting this one note
but somebody needs to tell her, I keep
trying to reach her with all my questions,
all my songs are really questions, why
does she keep singing, her voice climbs

out of my mouth like a reason to live,
why does she keep playing the grand
piano of my grief, why doesn't she just
go for a walk inside me and find the other
girls lost in other wings, doesn't she know
a woman can die from hearing her own
hurt, please—if somebody, anybody
out there can hear me—save her.

Diahann Carroll Takes a Bath at the Beverly Hills Hotel

This city remembered I was Black and said "no"
years before it came cooing with cash in hand,

so let the water rise until it splashes the marble.
Let them send a white girl to mop my flood later.

Tonight, I'm a love letter to all the women I've been,
a lyric for how I wear all my bodies. The fronds of palm

trees are burning outside my window, their agony
adds a twinkle to my champagne flute. I won't say

which part of this scene is a dream but all of it is deserved.
Let a wilderness grow around me. Let Julia cry with Claudine,

give them rough emeralds for each tear. Let Dominque undress Clara.
Let all my mothers swim in the river I've made for me and mine.

In our coolness, we birth anthems only we can hear. Hunters
mistake the chorus for a Black woman alone in a bathtub.

Let the pale reporters and their pointed questions about being
"the first and only" hang from trees like the warnings they are.

Grief #913

I grieve the boy I killed and the country fashioned out
of his bloodstains. I grieve that it was so easy. The knife,
lazy and confident, invading him. *This is what love feels like.*
I grieve that he believed me. Dumb animal, doe-eyed, ready-made
gift, just another border outlined in barbed wire and crime-scene chalk.
I grieve that, even then, I already knew I'd do it again, again, again,
again. I grieve a continent, nations united by the way terror turns
me on, the hot instant between thrust and gasp—"I want you"
and "I had you." Again, again, again, again. I grieve my face
onto the covers of history books. I grieve the descendants,
dumb animals, dead-eyed, ready-made gifts. *This is what love
requires.* I grieve that they believe me.

Saeed, or the Other One: II

The thing about those questions is that they follow you home. I was on the phone with my editor later that week, venting about that guy's question and all of that question's siblings, when I unlocked my door and dragged my suitcase into my apartment. Just before I reached for the light switch, I saw what looked like a dead body sprawled on the couch and I screamed and dropped my phone because that's exactly what we all do when we find dead bodies waiting for us in the dark in our living rooms after business trips.

"What's wrong? What's going on?" my editor yelled from the floor, but it was too late. I had already turned on the lights and there it was, a me that wasn't me, wearing my clothes. It looked up at me then, and I screamed so loud I started coughing.

My editor was screaming now too and, without taking my eyes off of whatever the living fuck was on my couch, I stooped down, sputtered some excuse about stubbing my toe, and hung up on her. While trying to stay as far away from the couch as I could while still being in the room, I looked him over, trying with mixed results not to scream or jump every time he blinked or took a breath.

To calm down, I settled in a far corner and limited myself to quick, darting glances. I realized he was doing the same thing and it started to feel silly: me in the corner of my living room and me on the couch in my living room, taking turns pretending not to be inspecting my selves. Soon, it was silly enough that I started to forget how terrified I had been just a few moments ago.

I heard myself think, "I would never hurt me," and he nodded because—I realize now though it didn't quite register in the moment—he was thinking the same thing. That's when I finally sat down on one of the chairs across from the couch. He smiled, impish and pleased, and I realized just how much I like my smile. I mean, I've always thought I had a good smile. It feels good and it looks good, but seeing him smiling with my smile made me happy in a way I had long forgotten I was capable of. It felt like being instantly unburdened of the memory of two-and-a-half griefs. That amount exactly.

Now, I still wasn't ready to talk but, feeling less afraid, I straightened my posture in the chair. He looked like the idea of myself coming into focus. At first, if you had asked me, I would've said he looked like a white policeman's description of me. Then I blinked and he was a Black policeman's description of me. Another blink and the me on the couch sharpened into a resemblance that could fool the neighbor who lived across the hallway, or the barista I saw most mornings at the coffee shop on the corner. Another blink and several aunties at my family reunion would've called him by my childhood nickname and happily fixed him a plate. We went on like that in a calm silence; I looked and he became. Before long, the differences between us were so subtle, I began to doubt their existence almost as soon as I noticed them.

That's when I took a breath and said, "Well, um, hello there," or "I guess I should say hi." I can't remember exactly because I was too distracted by the way I could feel the words leaving my mouth, one syllable at a time, drifting across the coffee table toward him. It's too dramatic to say that he ate them, but from the way he softly repeated my words, trying them out in the pause after I spoke, I believe that he couldn't actually speak until I first spoke to him. It was unnerving and then it wasn't. Something about being in his company—our company—had a way of immediately smoothing over rough edges as soon as I got to them. Just when I'd think "Well, that was weird," I'd think, "What was?"

—*continued*

"Whose house is this who did I hurt to get here and is it too late to call for help."

—Adam Falkner, The Willies

Alive at the End of the World

I hear the sirens and run
a hand over my silhouette,
surprised not to find bullet
wounds, burns, or history,

but now, ambered under
this streetlight, he pulls me in
for a kiss again and I decide,
briefly, to let the world kill

itself however it chooses: yes,
I hear the sirens and I am their
scream but tonight, I will moan
a future into my man's mouth.

"Sorry *as in* Pathetic"

Without a glance over her shoulder, a white woman walks
right through me to reach her next spike-heeled hour

and, in a life lived between breath and sigh, I wait for her
to mouth a quick *sorry,* nothing more, just a glance to say

I've been seen, but

                      once I was lost on a late-night street
and when I asked

the woman walking just ahead of me for help, she screamed
"Oh, god!" and clutched her purse the way the night holds me.

I told her I was sorry, then felt sorry for saying sorry.
I think of that woman often; I doubt she ever thinks of me.

A Stranger

I wonder if my dead mother still thinks of me.
I know I don't know her new name. I don't know

her, not now. I don't know if "her" is the word
burning in a stranger's mind when he sees my dead

mother walking down the street in her bright black
dress. I wonder if he inhales the cigarette smoke

that will eventually kill him and thinks, "I wish I knew
a woman who was both the light and every shadow

the light pierces." I wonder if a passing glance at my dead
mother is enough to make a poet out of anyone. I wonder

if I'm the song she hums as she waits for the light to change.

Okay, One More Story

Two blocks from home and already crying,
I tried not to scream when I pulled out a ring,
your favorite silver ring, instead of my keys,
and it // burned a memory into my palm so
I threw the ring to the ground and watched it
singe a perfect green circle of grass into the snow
where it fell //—no, there was no snow, never
any snow. But my mind keeps forcing a false
winter on me. You died in spring. I remember
that only the bowed heads of tulips got it right,
row after row of // red flowers found at the end
of an awful season which, if mixed into a potion
easily mistaken for poison, can give you back
the last three days of your life and keep you there
// but you were brain-dead and already dying.
Your fake silver ring had burned its last circle
onto your finger and the tulips outside bowed
their heads but not for you, no, not for you and—
forgive me—but I'm no longer the son I was
when I lost you, and I'd rather have you dead
than have you in that bed, dying forever.

Okay, One More Story

You died and a decade passed, then: one morning
everyone started dying.

Date Night

I meant to bring you flowers but when I reached
your door, all I had in my hands was teeth. Sorry,

I meant to say *grief*. Seems like all I say is *grief*.
Or *ghosts*. Or *please, don't leave*. Lately, I say it

in my mother's sleep. She used to cry and call out
her brother's name in her sleep. I've written about

this before. Grief, of course, but also, her sleep, but
also, her brother. He doesn't call me anymore. He

is my blood, and in a book I wrote but I don't think
he bothered to read. I grind my teeth in my sleep.

A man I used to sleep with told me I talk in my sleep
but blushed and held his tongue when I asked him

to say what I said in my sleep. When a Venus flytrap
flowers, the two white blossoms sit atop a very tall

stalk. Green teeth way down at the bottom. It's trying
to avoid triggering its own traps. It's trying to keep

the bees it needs for pollination away from its own traps.
I'm most dangerous when I'm hungry. I'm most hungry

when I'm hurting. Seems like I'm always hurting. Nothing
but teeth. Nothing but the same words calling out to me

in my sleep. Grief asking its ghosts not to leave. Please.
It's not up to me when I get to stop crying. Or hurting.

Or holding memories in my mouth, gentle as bees
I promised not to eat, but oh, the hurt is so sweet.

The Essential American Worker

America kills me, then says "now get back to work."

    [It's 7 p.m. again; it's time to clap.]

    [It's 7 p.m. again; it's time to clap.]

    [It's 7 p.m. again; it's time to clap.]

                                I know
a ghost like mine don't come cheap.

Against Progeny

Period. Already, at last I complete
my sentence & name myself the end

of me & any me that might be mirror-
drunk or legacy-sick enough to ask

for seconds or thirds. I bind this
body against the wish to multi-

ply my selves into an army of shoulda
beens, a swarm of still might bees.

I am the axe resting against this tree,
here where the sea has already laid

claim to the coast and the fault lines
have begun to grin. I want to quit

while I'm still ahead of all the hurts
that come next: someone with my blues

in their brain or my dark circling
their eyes, desperate to know why

I would inflict a drowned future on them.

A Difficult Love Song for Luther Vandross

Luther, sometimes lithe, is in the life.
Luther lives to work.
Luther's body of work is love songs.
Luther says his work is the love of his life.
Luther, larger lately, mostly means it.
Luther's body has a life of its own.
Luther doesn't love it.
Luther loves love but isn't known to be loving.
Luther's body knows he doesn't love it.
Luther confesses his body makes him hard to love.
Luther's body would say the problem is Luther.
Luther cries out for somebody to hold.
Luther means it.
Luther knows a song is not a body.
Luther says he has finally found somebody.
Luther and his body have a new love in their life.
Luther wants to look good for his love.
Luther makes his body obey his longing.
Luther giggles through all his interviews.
Luther leaves out pronouns when asked about his love.
Luther's new love leaves him.
Luther can't find the word *he*.
Luther sometimes sings *she*.
Luther doesn't mean it.
Luther prefers *you*.
Luther loves *you*.
Luther misses *you*.
Luther's body holds him when he sings.
Luther knows we request his love songs at our weddings.
Luther knows we love to hear him sing about *you*.

You won't sing a love song for Luther.

You could sing a love song for Luther but . . .

You wouldn't mean it.

You are nobody to Luther.

You are Luther's nobody to hold.

You are a love song Luther sings at somebody else's wedding.

You are an empty chair next to Luther at somebody else's wedding.

Nobody dances with Luther or his body at weddings.

Nobody sings a love song at Luther's wedding.

Nobody is at Luther's wedding.

Nobody, not *you*, not his body, not even Luther.

Little Richard Listens to Pat Boone Sing "Tutti Frutti"

If I could, and I bet I could, hell—I *know* I could
write a song that killed anyone who tried

to wrap their throat around it. I'm writing the first
verse right now, riding the rhythm like your mama

straddling the preacher while your daddy looks on
with a mouth full of every moan he can't have.

Ain't that what you really want? A stadium full
of white people screaming your stage name

and a smashed guitar where your dick used to be.
Ain't that what you deserve? God is the only reason

I haven't already held you down and spat the hook
into your mouth like a poison that will kill us both.

Grief #346

I grieve the men I swallowed like stolen pills.
I grieve the nights I tried and failed to purchase a second pair
of legs. A third. I grieve the ease with which I pulled bodies
into my body. I kept them all; I am crowded. I grieve the filth
of the twenty-dollar bill, the G-string's faded pink, the stench
of my want, the pit stain of my hunger. I grieve the lights on
at last call. I grieve your face, suddenly fluorescent lit. I grieve
the "sure." I grieve the "why not." The bodies I begged,
the bodies I borrowed, the bodies I broke and broke under.
I grieve snowfall on a ruined hand mirror. I grieve the men
I mistook for one another and the mistakes I mistook for men.
I grieve the bodies I thought beneath me and the body I became.
I grieve the dawns I killed and the days I slept through. I grieve
the sweat I left behind like a shadow. I grieve every name I called out
in the dark. I grieve that I never, not once, called out my own.

"Where did you come from?"

"I was hoping you would tell me."

"What are you?"

"I'm yours. Do you want me?"

"I—"

"You don't want me?"

"No, I do. I just—do you remember anything before I walked into the apartment?"

"I remember you saying that I needed you."

". . ."

"Well, actually you said *my pain . . . needs . . . me.*"

"Oh. Oh, shit."

"Yeah. Anyway, I heard it and came to find out why. Why do I need you?"

—*continued*

"Rescue me if I'm wrong."
—Frank B. Wilderson, *Afropessimism*

Alive at the End of the World

The End of the World was a nightclub.
Drag queens with machetes and rhinestoned

machine guns guarded the red and impassable
door on Friday nights. Just a look at the crowd,

all dressed up and swaying outside, made people
want to yell the truth about themselves to anyone

who'd listen, but no one heard. The End of the World
was loud. The End of the World leaked music

like radiation, and we loved the neon echo, even
though it taunted us or maybe because it taunted us:

kids leaning out of windows hours after bedtime,
cab drivers debating fares at the curb just for an excuse

to linger, pastors who'd pause at the corner and vow
that if they ever got inside, they'd burn it all down.

Extinction

Prey me long forgotten
before one of us swallows

the last bite of the last
good tomato in America.

Will future hungers ever
be sated by the sweet red

meat rotting in my hand?
I wonder if my killer has

loaned me time, musing
"Yes, I know he is mine

to mangle but they don't make
victims like him anymore.

Best not to rush." I wonder
if the fruit I'm bruising

is already somehow false,
a ripened memory ruined.

Everything Is Dying, Nothing Is Dead

It's a bright October morning
inside my annihilation

        and that song, the one hooked
in my ear like an heirloom loop, nears

the verse that always obliterates me
back into innocence

        while he hums
in the shower, rinsing last night

into the drain, as I rise to open a window
only to realize

        he's opened one for me already:

the autumn air has always been here,
lacing our every breath

    and I love the man who knows I love
the sweet-smoke smell of approaching death.

A Spell to Banish Grief

Only when you wake to a fistful of pulled hair
on the floor beside your bed and, from a glance,
can guess its weight, when you study dried tear
streaks on your cheeks like a farmer figuring out
where the season went wrong, when a friend calls
out your name three or four times before you know
your name is yours, when your name fits like clothes
you've suddenly outgrown, when there is too much
of you, too few of you, too you of you and the mirrors
wish all of you would just look away, when the clocks
can't feel their hands and the calendars begin to doubt
themselves, when you begin to agree with the glares
from mirrors but your reflection follows you around
the house anyway, when you catch yourself drunk
on memory, candles lit, eyes closed, your head tilted
in the direction of cemetery grass, yellow and balding
above what's left of the body that birthed you, and you
try to remember the sound of laughter in her throat
and fail, only then, orphan, will I take all my selves
and leave.

The Dead Dozens

Your grief is so heavy,
when we lowered the coffin,
all the pallbearers fell in too.

Your grief is so heavy,
when you cried your last good-bye, the end
of the world said "nigga, get off me!"

You love your mama so much,
Freud came back from the dead
just to study your sorry ass.

You love your mama so much,
when she died, our mamas died too.
Some of our favorite aunties caught strays.

I miss you so much,
I don't even use the word "hello" anymore.
Now, I greet everyone with "good-bye."

I miss you so much,
sometimes I go to strangers' funerals
and eulogize your ghost.

Your ghost cries so loud
our ancestors keep haunting me
to complain about the noise.

Your ghost cries so loud
I took my Black ass to a Klan rally
for some candle-lit peace and quiet.

After Watching a Video of Cicely Tyson Singing a Hymn,
I Realize I Wasn't a Good Grandson

Ma'am: lost-long son that I am,
I'm shrouded in enough mother-
echo to know I had what felt like

my reasons. But I've never lived
through a winter like this lonely
ruin before: the filth of clean-looking air

keeps claiming us, and I've got nothing
but time and this video of you singing
a hymn I couldn't hold in my mouth

if I tried. Cicely—I mean, Ma'am; sorry.
You don't know me from Adam. Neither
does my grandmother, and for good reason.

Performing as Miss Calypso, Maya Angelou Dances
Whenever She Forgets the Lyrics, which Billie Holiday,
Seated in the Audience, Finds Annoying

I killed a man once just by laughing.

We weren't even in the same city, but I felt his heart
stab itself like a star falling through me,

like the curve of my hips helping the crowd hear

this verse. Billie rolls her eyes just like she slurs
her words. She doesn't understand; I'll live forever

because nothing here matters. Lifetimes are just

costume jewelry. In the dressing room, Billie said
I'm going to be famous but it won't be for singing.

I plucked the best part of her curse out of her mouth
and pinned it to my blouse, another cheap jewel.

When I look at her, I see a girl who keeps mistaking dead ends

for mink stoles. I could pick her hurt out of any lineup.
That's why I laugh every time I look at her.

At 84 Years Old, Toni Morrison Wonders If She's Depressed

History pretends to forget itself
and memory bruises me back

into a burdened blue hour. My god,
the ghosts don't come quietly

anymore. Sweet headless laughter
used to scent my kitchen.

Every few moons, I'd find my father
made of tobacco smoke, his whisper

a guitar strum. A woman wrapped
in white lace walked out of the water

and waited patiently for her name.
But these new ghosts march through

me in mud-caked boots and smile
without teeth. I tell them to clean up

after themselves, and dead girls laugh
and leave behind bloody blue eyes.

All I Gotta Do Is Stay Black and Die (Apocalyptic Remix)

I don't know what's worse: your love
or your shadow, but nobody, not even me,

can outrun a sound: you're only here
because you shake the dust in all the empty

rooms of me, like a hymn I have good reason
not to hold, like a love song sung at somebody's

plantation wedding, like second- and third-
hand hurts bruised white as Hollywood.

Sorry, but I won't say which part of this scene
is a dream: the curve of my hip helping

you kill a cruel man under a family tree
or all of my bodies burning in a fun-house

mirror. Ain't that what you really want?
Ain't that what you deserve? Should've known

I'm nobody but a lyric for the ghosts quietly
growing around the mansion I've made

of me, like a wilderness of gardenias,
rough emeralds, and smashed guitars.

Grief #1

I grieve my early, pristine grief. The earth we piled
onto you, still soft and unsettled, the worms still at bay, the face
I remember still mostly your face. I grieve a living room sick
with the scent of farewell flowers, paper cuts from all those cards.
I grieve my body before my stomach recalled its hunger, before
my neck demanded a man breathing against it. Before all the empty
bottles, before loss began to calculate its profit margins. Simple grief,
innocent grief, grief unfamiliar with who I was before I started
grieving and who I would become after the sun set
on my last few minutes as your son.

Saeed, or The Other One: IV

The questions stung but never hurt. What hurt was how diffi-
cult it was to answer them, even alone in the warmth of our com-
pany. I don't know how long we sat in our living room, going back
and forth. At some point, I poured us some wine, then whiskey.
We got sushi delivered but barely touched it. We just couldn't
stop talking.

I'd answer his questions and then try to actually answer them
and fail, and then it would be his turn. We really tried to get to the
truth of my selves. But no matter how many ways we approached
the subject, we always ended up standing on its front lawn, con-
founded and without a key. I didn't know why he needed me, just
that he did. And the feeling was mutual. A white man in the audi-
ence with a white balloon of a blank stare had asked me about
my pain and there it was, an urgent tug in the ether. A call and
response inside the church of us.

The sky changed color and we paused to look at it, both a
bit puzzled because we couldn't tell if we were looking at dawn
or dusk. I picked up my glass, and just before I brought it to my
lips, I felt the sob coming a moment too late to stop it. I cried so
hard I didn't even notice how gently he had taken the glass out of
my hand. I didn't realize he had crowded into the chair with me
until I felt his arms wrapped around me. He kissed me on my wet
cheek, and I laughed because I didn't know what else to do.

It's possible I had been sputtering out my thoughts the entire
time but, feeling a little more coherent now, I started talking and
didn't stop until I was nearly panting because I needed him to
know that I had wanted to cry that night onstage. And it wasn't
the man's question, really. Well, it was, in a way. It's just that I
had been in the woods for so long and then I came to that man's
question and it was like a clearing. A little sunlit field overrun

with tall grass and all kinds of wildflowers I used to be able to name. And I could've done anything in that clearing. I could've danced in wild, erratic circles, or gathered flowers for a crown, or lain down and rested, or yelled out the names of everyone I loved and missed. I could've marched right into the middle of that field and listed my hurts one by one until I was free of them. Anything. I could've done anything. But instead, I turned around and went back into the woods. That's what I always did. I went back into the woods.

My words blended with the brightening light drifting in from the window. I paused then, unsure if I had been talking or thinking. He nodded as if to say *yes*. And it felt so good being known, I almost cried again.

"They want to see me in that clearing. Maybe they think I need it or they need it or maybe they just want it," I said finally. "But I don't want to go out there for them."

We sat in silence, both tired and a bit relieved. And then, mushed into that chair as we were, his cheek was still against my cheek, and I felt the muscles in his face moving the way they do when we're about to make a joke.

"Well," he said, gently feeling his way into the setup, "I could be you out there, for a little while. I mean, I'm pretty good at it." I chuckled, and we slid back into silence, already picturing him onstage with my words in his mouth.

—continued.

Notes at the End of the World

That's Not Snow, It's Ash, in a way, is the quiet, bewildered heart of the book. I wish someone had warned me that the end of the world could look like a peaceful Saturday morning.

If You Had an Off Button, I'd Name You "Off" was inspired by a February 2020 *Digit* article titled "Japanese Scientists Create Robot Child That Can 'Feel' Pain." The quote that begins "Here in Japan, we believe . . ." was stated by Dr. Minoru Asada, the lead researcher on the Affetto project. I do not know if Dr. Asada has a son or is married. I do not know what Affetto thinks about when he's left alone in the dark.

All I Gotta Do Is Stay Black and Die was inspired by the news of comedian Paul Mooney's death on May 19, 2021.

It's 1975 and Paul Mooney Says "Nigger" a Hundred Times gets its title and opening line from a joke Paul Mooney makes on his *Race* album. It's inspired by his frustration after being interviewed by Lorne Michaels. Mooney mined that frustration to write the famous "Word Association" sketch for Richard Pryor and Chevy Chase. All of the images in the poem reference specific Paul Mooney jokes except for the one about Chevy Chase's dick. That one is on the house.

Deleted Voice Message: Hey, Robyn—It's Me, Whitney was inspired by Robyn Crawford's memoir *A Song for You: My Life with Whitney Houston* and Kevin Macdonald's 2018 documentary *Whitney*. In *A Song for You*, Crawford writes about accidentally deleting a phone message after a few seconds before getting to hear the entire message: "When I heard that tone, her voice was different. The way she said my name: 'Robyn.' She says this very softly." It was the only part of the message she heard. And later: "I wish I'd found a way to get to her. But she was waiting for me, and I was waiting for her."

Grief #213 was inspired by a 2015 essay I wrote for BuzzFeed News titled "Self-Portrait as an Ungrateful Black Writer."

Heritage is a nonfiction poem about a stop in Oxford, Mississippi, during my 2019 book tour for *How We Fight for Our Lives*. The essay on lynching is "The Great American Press Release" by Maurice Carlos Ruffin and appears in the September 2019 issue of the *Oxford American*. The morning after reading Ruffin's essay, I woke up to learn that President Donald Trump had just published a tweet likening the House impeachment inquiry against him to a lynching.

After the School Board Meeting changes color every time I check the news. Though the initial inspiration owes a debt to *The Nickel Boys* by Colson Whitehead, the poem was also written with the Columbus-area neighborhood Upper Arlington in mind. In 1955, UA's high school was built on top of a historically Black cemetery. In 2020, as construction started on a new building for the school, the district uncovered six graves dating back nearly two hundred years. By the fall of 2021, news stories about white parents loudly decrying "critical race theory" had become unavoidable.

Black Ice is a nonfiction poem and, as it happened, was written a month before an especially perilous winter storm caused calamity throughout the state of Texas in March 2021.

The Trial was written with George Floyd and Darnella Frazier in mind, in particular. One of the many trials Black people endure is the violent repetition of police brutality and images of that brutality. I wrote the first draft of the poem the morning of June 11, 2021; that afternoon, Darnella Frazier was awarded a Pulitzer Prize Special Citation "for courageously recording the murder of George Floyd." She was seventeen years old the day Floyd was murdered.

Aretha Franklin Hears an Echo While Singing "Save Me" was inspired by David Ritz's book *Respect: The Life of Aretha Franklin*.

Diahann Carroll Takes a Bath at the Beverly Hills Hotel was inspired by a 2009 career retrospective moderated by Anthony DeSantis. While filming the television show *Julia* in 1968, Diahann Caroll lived in the Beverly Hills Hotel. A September 2021 article in *The Atlantic* by Hannah Giorgis notes that Caroll later admitted that "the stress of playing a role [on *Julia*] so removed from the Black life she knew had made her physically ill."

Grief #913 was written in Columbus, Ohio, in a nation made of stolen land.

Alive at the End of the World echoes "Those Winter Sundays" by Robert Hayden.

"Sorry *as in* Pathetic" is a nonfiction poem.

Okay, One More Story is dedicated to my mother, Carol Sweet-Jones.

Okay, One More Story is dedicated to the tenth anniversary of my mother's death.

Date Night references my memoir *How We Fight for Our Lives* as well as the afterlife of the experience of publishing that book which, I suppose, could be said for this book as well. You don't get to decide when an experience is done with you.

The Essential American Worker was inspired by capitalism and the pandemic. The white space in the poem is ghost text as opposed to blank space.

A Difficult Love Song for Luther Vandross was inspired by Craig Seymour's excellent biography *Luther: The Life and Longing of Luther Vandross*. The poem is intended to be difficult to read out loud as a nod to the fact that Vandross was notoriously exacting about enunciation of lyrics and would regularly interrupt his collaborators in the studio if he felt that they hadn't gotten a word right.

Little Richard Listens to Pat Boone Sing "Tutti Frutti" was inspired by the rage behind Little Richard's iconic screams. In America, one way to suffer a death before you die is to mean so much to so many people for so many different reasons. It's not just that we could hear James Brown's shouts in Little Richard's screams, or see Prince's ass in Little Richard's curves. It's that Bob Dylan wrote in his high school yearbook that his life's ambition was "to join Little Richard." It's that Pat Boone watered down and added bleach to "Tutti Frutti" and it was a bigger hit than Little Richard's original version. It's that Pat Boone did it again with "Long Tall Sally." It's that because of a shitty contract Little Richard signed, he only made half a cent for every record of "Tutti Frutti" that sold. It's that, for Little Richard, selling more than half a million copies of "Tutti Frutti" amounted to a mere $25,000 in his bank account. It's that when Little Richard said, "If Elvis is the King of Rock 'n' Roll, I'm the queen," he wasn't being cute or sassy; he was correcting the historical record and demanding equity that he never received. In America, one way to suffer a death before you die is for people to applaud you even as they steal from you. In America, one way to suffer a death before you die is to be an "inspiration" to white male rock stars. There should be catacombs under the Rock & Roll Hall of Fame. Little Richard alone would account for at least a dozen tombs.

Alive at the End of the World is dedicated to victims of the Pulse nightclub shooting.

Extinction was supposed to be a happy, carpe diem kind of poem.

A Spell to Banish Grief was inspired by a depressive episode in January 2021 during which I realized I was pulling out my hair in my sleep.

The Dead Dozens should be read while playing a game of Spades that ends in drunk laughter and an act of unspeakable violence.

After Watching a Video of Cicely Tyson Singing a Hymn, I Realize I Wasn't a Good Grandson was inspired by a YouTube clip featuring Cicely Tyson performing a scene in *The Trip to Bountiful*.

Performing as Miss Calypso, Maya Angelou Dances Whenever She Forgets the Lyrics, which Billie Holliday, Seated in the Audience, Finds Annoying was inspired by a series of encounters between the two icons in the late 1950s, just before Holliday died. Angelou eventually documented the encounters in her 1981 memoir *The Heart of a Woman*. Arguably, Holliday was right. After recording one album as Miss Calypso, Angelou abandoned her music career.

At 84 Years Old, Toni Morrison Wonders If She's Depressed references *Song of Solomon, Beloved,* and *The Bluest Eye*. In an April 2015 interview with Terry Gross for NPR's *Fresh Air*, Morrison admitted, "I guess I'm depressed. [*laughs*] I don't know. I can't explain it. Part of it is the irritability of being eighty-four, and part of it is being not as physically strong as I once was. And part of it is my misunderstanding, I think, of what's going on in the world."

All I Gotta Do Is Stay Black and Die (Apocalyptic Remix) is a found poem built from lines that appear throughout the "All I Gotta Do Is Stay Black and Die" sequence that forms the spine of the book.

Grief #1 is a nonfiction poem.

Acknowledgments

Thank you to the editors who published versions of these poems in their pages:

Tin House: "Grief #913"

The New Yorker: "A Stranger," "Alive at the End of the World," "A Spell to Banish Grief"

Vox: "After the School Board Meeting"

Mumber: "Diahann Carroll Takes a Bath at the Beverly Hills Hotel"

Oxford-American: "Saeed, or The Other One"

Coffee House Press began as a small letterpress operation in 1972 and has grown into an internationally renowned nonprofit publisher of literary fiction, essay, poetry, and other work that doesn't fit neatly into genre categories.

Coffee House is both a publisher and an arts organization. Through our *Books in Action* program and publications, we've become interdisciplinary collaborators and incubators for new work and audience experiences. Our vision for the future is one where a publisher is a catalyst and connector.

LITERATURE
is not the same thing as
PUBLISHING

Funder Acknowledgments

Coffee House Press is an internationally renowned independent book publisher and arts nonprofit based in Minneapolis, MN; through its literary publications and Books in Action program, Coffee House acts as a catalyst and connector—between authors and readers, ideas and resources, creativity and community, inspiration and action.

Coffee House Press books are made possible through the generous support of grants and donations from corporations, state and federal grant programs, family foundations, and the many individuals who believe in the transformational power of literature. This activity is made possible by the voters of Minnesota through a Minnesota State Arts Board Operating Support grant, thanks to the legislative appropriation from the Arts and Cultural Heritage Fund. Coffee House also receives major operating support from the Amazon Literary Partnership, Jerome Foundation, McKnight Foundation, Target Foundation, and the National Endowment for the Arts (NEA). To find out more about how NEA grants impact individuals and communities, visit www.arts.gov.

Coffee House Press receives additional support from Bookmobile; Dorsey & Whitney LLP; Elmer L. & Eleanor J. Andersen Foundation; Fredrikson & Byron, P.A.; the Matching Grant Program Fund of the Minneapolis Foundation; Mr. Pancks' Fund in memory of Graham Kimpton; the Schwab Charitable Fund; and the U.S. Bank Foundation.

The Publisher's Circle of Coffee House Press

Publisher's Circle members make significant contributions to Coffee House Press's annual giving campaign. Understanding that a strong financial base is necessary for the press to meet the challenges and opportunities that arise each year, this group plays a crucial part in the success of Coffee House's mission.

Recent Publisher's Circle members include many anonymous donors, Patricia A. Beithon, Anitra Budd, Andrew Brantingham, Dave & Kelli Cloutier, Mary Ebert & Paul Stembler, Jocelyn Hale & Glenn Miller, the Rehael Fund-Roger Hale/Nor Hall of the Minneapolis Foundation, Randy Hartten & Ron Lotz, Dylan Hicks & Nina Hale, William Hardacker, Kenneth & Susan Kahn, Stephen & Isabel Keating, the Kenneth Koch Literary Estate, Cinda Kornblum, Jennifer Kwon Dobbs & Stefan Liess, the Lambert Family Foundation, the Lenfestey Family Foundation, Sarah Lutman & Rob Rudolph, the Carol & Aaron Mack Charitable Fund of the Minneapolis Foundation, Gillian McCain, Malcolm S. McDermid & Katie Windle, Mary & Malcolm McDermid, Daniel N. Smith III & Maureen Millea Smith, Peter Nelson & Jennifer Swenson, Enrique & Jennifer Olivarez, Alan Polsky, Robin Preble, Jeffrey Sugerman & Sarah Schultz, Nan G. Swid, Grant Wood, and Margaret Wurtele.

For more information about the Publisher's Circle and other ways to support Coffee House Press books, authors, and activities, please visit www.coffeehousepress.org/pages/donate or contact us at info@coffeehousepress.org.

Saeed Jones was born in Memphis, Tennessee, and grew up in Lewisville, Texas. His work has appeared in the *New Yorker,* the *New York Times,* and *GQ,* and he has been featured on public radio programs including NPR's *Fresh Air, Pop Culture Happy Hour, It's Been A Minute with Sam Sanders,* and *All Things Considered.* He lives in Columbus, Ohio, with his dog, Caesar, and tweets @TheFerocity.

Alive at the End of the World was designed by
Bookmobile Design & Digital Publisher Services.
Text is set in Iowan Old Style.